cakes

Ivy Press

cakes

25 mouthwatering recipes

Susanna Tee

First published in 2008 by

Ivy Press
The Old Candlemakers
West Street, Lewes
East Sussex BN7 2NZ, UK
www.ivy-group.co.uk

ISBN-13: 978-1-905695-71-3
ISBN-10: 1-905695-71-3

Printed in China

10 9 8 7 6 5 4 3 2 1

Ivy Press
This book was conceived, designed
and produced by Ivy Press.

Creative Director Peter Bridgewater
Publisher Jason Hook
Editorial Director Caroline Earle
Art Director Clare Harris
Senior Editor Lorraine Turner
Senior Art Editor Sarah Howerd
Project Designer Kate Haynes
Publishing Assistant Katie Ellis
Concept Design 'Ome Design
Photographer Jeremy Hopley
Food Stylist Susanna Tee

contents

introduction

There are not many things as tantalising as the smell of home-baking, and a slice of freshly baked cake is a delicious treat. The best thing of all is that it doesn't just have to be for a birthday or other special occasion.

It is very satisfying to produce a cake for when the children come home from school, and when friends join you for a mid-morning coffee or a cup of afternoon tea. Then there is the trestle table, laden with home-made cakes, at the local summer fête, where it is always the star attraction. The spectacular chocolate cake or moist cake served with fresh fruit as a dessert cannot be forgotten, and a home-made cake given as a gift is always appreciated.

Cake baking is an age-old tradition and today, despite our busy lifestyles, it is comforting and nostalgic to produce something so appealing. It is also good to know that what you have baked is made from wholesome, natural ingredients, and the flavour far surpasses any purchased variety.

The history of the cake goes back a long way. The word 'cake' derives from the Viking word *kaka*, and the art of cake making can be traced back to ancient Egypt, where a cake was similar to unleavened bread. Over the years, sugar, spices, chocolate and baking powder were added so that today we have the cake as we know it.

Imagine your favourite cake. Whether a humble teabread, a luxurious chocolate cake or a sumptuous fruit creation, it can be found in this collection of recipes. Cakes are fun and easy to make: it takes no time to rustle up a cake, fill the kitchen with mouthwatering aromas and feel proud of your creation. Home-made cakes can be kept in an air-tight container or tin for two to three days, and light fruit cakes will keep for up to one month – but you will find that they disappear long before that.

the basics

To make a cake, you need only a few basic ingredients and, apart from cake tins, you require very little special equipment. Simply follow these useful tips and you will be guaranteed a successful cake every time.

Flour, sugar, fat and eggs and the basic ingredients of cake making. The flour may be plain or self-raising, but if you need self-raising flour and have only plain, you can make it by sifting 2½ teaspoons of baking powder into every 225 g/8 oz plain flour.

Butter or margarine is suggested in the recipes, butter for taste and richness but, should you wish to cut the cost, there is no reason not to use a hard margarine. Soft margarines also give good results and can save time too. For a basic mixture, simply put the soft tub margarine, flour, sugar and eggs in a bowl and, using an electric whisk, beat together until well combined.

Caster sugar is recommended because it dissolves more easily than granulated sugar, and large eggs are used unless otherwise stated. Ideally, use eggs at room temperature because cold eggs tend to curdle the mixture. This can result in a tough cake.

When cakes are made by the creaming method of whisking the butter and sugar together, it is best to use an electric whisk to incorporate as much air as possible into the mixture. This produces a light cake when baked but, if you haven't got an electric whisk, you can beat the mixture with a wood spoon until pale in colour, and light and fluffy in texture.

Useful tips

- Preheat the oven prior to baking despite any oven manufacturer's instructions to the contrary. If you have a fan-assisted oven, reduce the temperature according to its instruction manual.

- If you haven't got the correct size cake tin that is specified in the recipe, a quantity of cake mixture designed for a round cake tin will fill a 2.5 cm/1 in smaller square cake tin and vice versa. The same quantity of cake mixture used in a 900 g/2 lb loaf tin can be baked in a deep, round 18 cm/7 in cake tin.

- Line the cake tins before you begin making the cake because, once you have added liquid to self-raising flour, the raising agents in the flour start to activate and it is important to bake the cake as soon as it is prepared.

- Keep butter or margarine wrappers: fold and store in the refrigerator and use to grease cake tins.

- Bake the cake in the centre of the oven but, when baking two cakes, change them round halfway through the cooking time.

- Do not open the oven door during the first half of the cooking time because cold air may cause the cake to sink in the centre.

a feast of cakes

teatime treats

sticky gingerbread

carrot cake

coffee walnut cake

apricot teabread

caraway seed cake

pine kernel teabread

walnut cake

rich fruit cake

dried fruit ring cake

chocolate favourites

chocolate fudge cake

sachertorte

death by chocolate

marble cake

devil's food cake

black forest gâteau

chocolate brownies

chocolate crispy cakes

fruit sensations

lemon polenta cake

almond apple cake

banana teabread

fresh orange cake

lemon drizzle cake

raspberry streusel cake

vanilla sponge cake

cherry cake

sticky gingerbread

Dark, rich and sticky are the qualities of good gingerbread and, if you can resist the temptation, it gets even better the longer that it is kept. It's perfect with a cup of tea in the afternoon.

makes 9 squares

you will need

4 pieces stem ginger

150 g/5½ oz butter or hard margarine, plus extra for greasing

100 g/3½ oz dark soft brown sugar

115 g/4 oz black treacle

115 g/4 oz golden syrup

2 large eggs

225 g/8 oz plain white flour

2 tsp ground ginger

1 tsp bicarbonate of soda

2 tbsp milk

butter, to serve

1 Preheat the oven to 180°C/350°F/Gas Mark 4. Grease a square 20 cm/8 in cake tin with butter and line with baking paper. Finely chop the stem ginger and set aside.

2 Put the butter and sugar in a large bowl and, using an electric whisk, beat together until pale and fluffy. Add the black treacle and golden syrup and beat together.

3 Beat the eggs in a bowl, then add to the mixture a little at a time, and beat together until incorporated. Sift the flour and ground ginger into the mixture and beat together until well mixed. Stir the bicarbonate of soda into the milk, then beat into the mixture. Stir in the chopped ginger. Turn the mixture into the prepared tin and spread out evenly.

4 Bake the cake in the oven for 40–45 minutes, or until the top is firm but the centre just set. Do not overcook but allow it to remain sticky. It will continue to cook slightly as it cools. Leave to cool in the tin.

5 Ideally, wrap the gingerbread in baking paper and then in foil and store in an airtight container for 2–3 days to mature before eating. Cut into squares and spread with butter, to serve.

carrot cake

Carrots have been used in cakes since medieval times to add sweetness. The result is a moist, sweet cake, which is very popular in Switzerland. There you can buy marzipan carrots for decoration, but walnuts are good too.

makes 15 squares

you will need

butter, for greasing
100 g/3½ oz walnut halves
450 g/1 lb caster sugar
350 ml/12 fl oz sunflower oil
4 large eggs, separated
75 ml/2½ fl oz hot water
300 g/10½ oz plain white flour
½ tsp baking powder
½ tsp bicarbonate of soda
2½ tsp mixed ground spice
225 g/8 oz carrots
50 g/1¾ oz sultanas or raisins
walnut halves, to decorate

for the icing

85 g/3 oz full-fat cream cheese
40 g/1½ oz butter, softened
1 tsp vanilla extract
450 g/1 lb icing sugar

1 Preheat the oven to 180°C/350°F/Gas Mark 4. Grease a 46 x 20 cm/18 x 8 in roasting tin with butter and line with baking paper.

2 Roughly chop the walnuts. Put the sugar and oil in a large bowl and beat together with a wooden spoon. Beat the egg yolks into the mixture, then beat in the hot water.

3 Sift the flour, baking powder, bicarbonate of soda and spice into the bowl, then beat the mixture together until smooth. Finely grate the carrots into the mixture. Add the chopped walnuts and sultanas and stir together. Whisk the egg whites until stiff and then, using a large metal spoon, fold into the mixture. Turn the mixture into the prepared tin and spread out evenly.

4 Bake the cake in the oven for about 1 hour, or until well risen and golden brown. Leave to cool in the tin.

5 Meanwhile, make the icing. Put the cream cheese, butter and vanilla extract in a large bowl; beat together until smooth. Sift in the icing sugar, then beat together until combined. When the cake is cold, spread the icing generously on top of the cake. Cut into squares and top each one with a walnut half (or a maripan carrot if you manage to find them).

coffee walnut cake

Coffee and walnuts are a great combination and this cake, filled and topped with coffee butter cream, is always enticing. It makes the perfect coffee-time treat. The coffee extract really brings out the coffee flavour.

serves 8

you will need

100 g/3½ oz shelled walnuts

175 g/6 oz butter or hard margarine, softened, plus extra for greasing

175 g/6 oz caster sugar

3 large eggs

2 tbsp chicory and coffee extract

175 g/6 oz white self-raising flour

1½ tsp baking powder

chocolate-coated coffee beans, to decorate

for the butter cream

350 g/12 oz butter, softened

175 g/6 oz icing sugar

3 tbsp milk

1 tbsp chicory and coffee extract

1 Preheat the oven to 160°C/325°F/Gas Mark 3. Grease two 20 cm/8 in sandwich tins with butter and line with baking paper. Reserve 8 whole walnuts and finely chop the remaining nuts.

2 Put the butter and sugar in a large bowl and, using an electric whisk, beat together until pale and fluffy. Beat the eggs in a small bowl and beat into the mixture a little at a time until mixed. Beat in the chicory and coffee extract.

3 Sift the flour and baking powder into the mixture and fold in until incorporated and then fold in the chopped walnuts. Turn the mixture into the prepared tins and spread out evenly.

4 Bake the cakes for 35–40 minutes, or until well risen and firm to the touch. Turn out of the tins and cool on a wire rack.

5 To make the butter cream, put the butter in a large bowl, sift in the icing sugar, add the milk, and chicory and coffee extract, and beat together with a wooden spoon until smooth.

6 When the cakes are cold, use some of the butter cream to sandwich the cake halves together. Spread the remainder over the top, pulling it into swirls to look attractive. Decorate with the reserved walnut halves and coffee beans.

apricot teabread

This is an excellent, moist fruit bread and apart from being enjoyed at coffee or teatime, it is also good when spread with butter and perhaps honey and served for breakfast.

serves 10–12

you will need

175 g/6 oz dried apricots

225 ml/8 fl oz fresh orange juice

55 g/2 oz walnuts

350 g/12 oz self-raising white flour

1 tsp ground cinnamon

115 g/4 oz butter or hard margarine, cut into cubes, plus extra for greasing

85 g/3 oz caster sugar

2 large eggs

icing sugar, to decorate

1 Using scissors, snip the apricots into small pieces and put in a bowl. Add the orange juice and leave to soak for 3–4 hours or overnight.

2 Preheat the oven to 180°C/350°F/Gas Mark 4. Grease a 900 g/2 lb loaf tin with butter and line with baking paper.

3 Roughly chop the walnuts. Sift the flour and cinnamon together into a large bowl. Add the butter and rub in with your fingers until the mixture resembles fine breadcrumbs. Alternatively, put the flour and butter in a food processor and blend together, using a pulsating action, to form fine breadcrumbs.

4 Add the chopped walnuts and sugar to the mixture and stir together until well mixed. Add the soaked apricots and their juice. Beat the eggs in a bowl, then add to the mixture a little at a time, and beat together until incorporated. Turn the mixture into the prepared tin and spread out evenly.

5 Bake the cake in the oven for about 1 hour, or until golden brown and firm to the touch. Leave in the tin for 5 minutes to cool slightly, then turn out of the tin and leave to cool on a wire rack. Serve dusted with sifted icing sugar to decorate.

caraway seed cake

Caraway seed cake is a classic old English cake that was traditionally served at teatime. Lemon juice and a lemon butter icing has been added to this recipe, which gives the cake an additional refreshing flavour.

serves 6–8

you will need

175 g/6 oz butter or hard margarine, softened, plus extra for greasing

175 g/6 oz caster sugar

3 large eggs

1 large lemon

175 g/6 oz self-raising white flour

2 tsp caraway seeds

for the icing

100 g/3½ oz butter, softened

125 g/4½ oz icing sugar

1 small lemon

1 Preheat the oven to 180°C/350°F/Gas Mark 4. Grease a deep, round 18 cm/7 in cake tin with butter and line with baking paper. Put the butter and sugar in a large bowl and, using an electric whisk, beat together until pale and fluffy. Beat the eggs in a bowl, then add to the mixture a little at a time, and beat together until incorporated.

2 Finely grate the lemon rind into the mixture. Squeeze the juice from the lemon and add to the mixture with the flour and caraway seeds and beat together until well mixed. Turn the mixture into the prepared tin and spread out evenly.

3 Bake the cake for 50 minutes, or until golden brown and firm to the touch. Turn out of the tin and leave to cool on a wire rack.

4 Meanwhile, make the icing. Put the butter in a large bowl. Sift in the icing sugar and beat together with a wooden spoon until smooth. Finely grate the lemon rind into the mixture, then squeeze the juice from the lemon and add 1 tablespoon to the mixture and beat together.

5 When the cake is cold, spread the icing on top to cover the cake and, using a palette knife, swirl to look attractive.

pine kernel teabread

This moist teabread, flavoured with lemon and dotted with pine kernels, is a sophisticated cake to serve at any time of day. It is also ideal for buffets and picnics, or why not pack a slice into a lunchbox?

serves 10–12

you will need

50 g/1¾ oz pine kernels

1 large lemon

250 g/9 oz butter or hard margarine, softened, plus extra for greasing

225 g/8 oz caster sugar

4 large eggs

100 g/3½ oz plain white flour

115 g/4 oz ground almonds

1 Preheat the oven to 180°C/350°F/Gas Mark 4. Grease a 900 g/2 lb loaf tin with butter and line with baking paper. Roughly chop half of the pine kernels. Finely grate the rind and squeeze the juice of the lemon. Set aside.

2 Put the butter and sugar in a large bowl and, using an electric whisk, beat together until pale and fluffy.

3 Beat the eggs in a bowl, then add to the mixture a little at a time, and beat together until incorporated.

4 Add the chopped pine kernels, the lemon rind and juice, the flour and ground almonds to the mixture and fold in until well combined.

5 Turn the mixture into the prepared tin and spread out evenly. Sprinkle the remaining pine kernels on top.

6 Bake the cake in the oven for 50–60 minutes, or until golden brown and a skewer inserted in the centre comes out clean. Leave to cool in the tin before removing.

walnut cake

This is a popular cake in Italy, where walnuts grow in abundance, and is particularly rich and moist. An Italian espresso coffee would be the perfect accompaniment to serve with it.

serves 10

you will need

butter, for greasing

250 g/9 oz walnut halves

6 large eggs, separated

250 g/9 oz caster sugar

55 g/2 oz plain white flour

1 tsp baking powder

icing sugar, to decorate

whipped double cream, to serve

1 Preheat the oven to 150°C/300°F/Gas Mark 2. Grease a round, deep 23 cm/9 in cake tin with butter and line with baking paper. Put the walnuts in a food processor and, using a pulsating action, finely chop.

2 Put the egg yolks and half the sugar in a large bowl and, using an electric whisk, beat together until pale and fluffy.

3 Sift the flour and baking powder into the mixture and mix together until combined. Gradually beat in the remaining sugar and then, using a large metal spoon, fold in the chopped nuts.

4 Whisk the egg whites until stiff, then fold into the mixture. Turn the mixture into the prepared tin and spread out evenly.

5 Bake the cake in the oven for about 1½ hours, or until firm to the touch. Remove the cake from the tin and leave to cool on a wire rack.

6 Before serving, dust the cake with sifted icing sugar and serve with whipped cream.

rich fruit cake

The secret of this recipe is that the fruit is soaked prior to baking, making it moist. It is also versatile: suitable for a Christmas cake if iced, or a Dundee cake if topped with almonds. It is delicious served with a crumbly cheese.

serves 10

you will need

500 g/1 lb 2 oz mixed dried fruit

225 ml/8 fl oz sherry, brandy or fresh orange juice

225 g/8 oz butter or hard margarine, plus extra for greasing

225 g/8 oz soft light brown sugar

4 large eggs

280 g/10 oz plain white flour

55 g/2 oz blanched almonds or walnut halves

85 g/3 oz glacé cherries

40 g/1½ oz blanched almonds or 450 g/1 lb marzipan and 675 g/1 lb 8 oz royal icing, to decorate if desired

1 Put the dried fruit in a large bowl. Add the sherry and leave to soak for 24 hours or overnight, stirring occasionally.

2 Preheat the oven to 160°C/325°F/Gas Mark 3. Grease a deep, round 20 cm/8 in cake tin with butter and line with baking paper. Put the butter and sugar in a large bowl and, using an electric whisk, beat together until pale and fluffy.

3 Beat the eggs in a small bowl, then add to the mixture a little at a time, and beat together until incorporated. Add the flour and, using a large metal spoon, fold in until incorporated.

4 Add the soaked fruit and liquid, the almonds and the cherries to the mixture and fold in until well mixed. Turn the mixture into the prepared tin, spread out evenly and make a slight indentation in the centre with the back of the spoon. If wished, arrange the second batch of almonds on the top.

5 Bake the cake for 2½ hours, or until a skewer inserted in the centre comes out clean. If browning too much after 1½ hours, cover the surface with a thick layer of baking paper. Leave to cool in the tin. If storing, wrap in baking paper and then in foil. If wished, cover with marzipan and royal icing to decorate.

dried fruit ring cake

It makes a change to bake a cake in a ring mould and you can ring the changes too with this recipe. Although the recipe suggests dates and raisins, you could use other dried fruits, such as apricots, figs and sultanas.

you will need

140 g/5 oz dried dates

225 g/8 oz butter or hard margarine, softened, plus extra for greasing

200 g/7 oz caster sugar

4 large eggs, separated

225 g/8 oz plain white flour

2 tsp ground cinnamon

85 g/3 oz raisins

icing sugar, to decorate

1 Preheat the oven to 200°C/400°F/Gas Mark 6. Grease a 20 cm/8 in ring mould with butter. Using scissors, cut the dates into small pieces.

2 Put the butter and sugar in a large bowl and, using an electric whisk, beat together until pale and fluffy. Add the egg yolks and beat together.

3 Sift the flour and cinnamon into the bowl. Add the chopped dates and the raisins and beat together until well mixed.

4 Whisk the egg whites until stiff and standing in soft peaks and then, using a large metal spoon, fold into the mixture. Turn the mixture into the prepared tin and spread out evenly.

5 Bake the cake in the oven for about 30 minutes, or until a skewer inserted in the cake comes out clean. Turn out of the tin and leave to cool on a wire rack. When cold, dust with sifted icing sugar to decorate.

chocolate fudge cake

The unconventional way of cooking this cake at such a low temperature and with a bain marie in the oven, makes it the most moist, chocolaty, fudgy cake in the world. In other words, it is totally irresistible.

you will need

175 g/6 oz butter or hard margarine, softened, plus extra for greasing

175 g/6 oz caster sugar

4 large eggs

225 g/8 oz drinking-chocolate powder

85 g/3 oz self-raising white flour

icing sugar, to decorate

for the filling

85 g/3 oz butter, softened

85 g/3 oz icing sugar

1. Preheat the oven to 140°C/275°F/Gas Mark 1. Put a roasting tin, filled with hot water, on the bottom shelf of the oven. Grease two 20 cm/8 in sandwich tins with butter and line with baking paper. Put the butter and sugar in a large bowl and, using an electric whisk, beat together until pale and fluffy.

2. Beat the eggs in a bowl and beat into the mixture a little at a time. Add the drinking-chocolate powder and flour to the mixture and fold in until well combined. Turn the mixture into the prepared tins and spread out evenly.

3. Bake the cakes for 1 hour. Then turn off the heat but leave the cakes in the oven for a further 30 minutes. Remove from the oven, then turn out of the tin and leave to cool on a wire rack.

4. Meanwhile, make the filling. Put the butter in a large bowl. Sift in the icing sugar and beat together with a wooden spoon until smooth. (Don't be tempted to use an electric whisk, or you will be covered in a cloud of icing sugar.)

5. When the cakes are cold, remove from the tins and sandwich together with the filling. Dust with sifted icing sugar.

sachertorte

This famous Austrian cake, created more than 175 years ago and served at the Hotel Sacher in Vienna, closely resembles the original. Traditionally it is accompanied by whipped cream and served with coffee.

serves 10

you will need

100 g/3½ oz good-quality plain chocolate, broken into pieces

115 g/4 oz butter, softened, plus extra for greasing

115 g/4 oz caster sugar

4 large eggs

115 g/4 oz ground almonds

55 g/2 oz fresh, fine brown breadcrumbs

3 tbsp apricot glaze

whipped cream, to serve

for the topping

100 g/3½ oz good-quality plain chocolate

55 g/2 oz butter

55 g/2 oz icing sugar

1 tsp hot water

1 Preheat the oven to 180°C/350°F/Gas Mark 4. Grease and line a round 23 cm/9 in spring-release cake tin. Put the chocolate into a heatproof bowl set over a saucepan of simmering water, and heat gently until melted. Remove from the heat.

2 Put the butter and sugar in a large bowl and, using an electric whisk, beat together until pale and fluffy. Mix in the melted chocolate. Separate the eggs: beat the yolks into the chocolate mixture and put the whites in a clean bowl. Mix the almonds and breadcrumbs into the chocolate mixture. Whisk the egg whites until stiff, then fold into the mixture. Turn the mixture into the prepared tin and spread out evenly.

3 Bake the cake in the oven for 40–45 minutes, or until firm to the touch. Leave to cool in the tin. When cold, remove from the tin and spread the apricot glaze on top.

4 For the topping, melt the chocolate and butter in a heatproof bowl set over a pan of simmering water. Remove from the heat, stir, sift in the icing sugar and mix well. Stir in the water, leave for 5 minutes, then spread over the cake. When it begins to set, use a skewer to write 'Sacher' on top. Leave to set.

death by chocolate

The name of this cake, also known as American Fudge Cake, indicates just how unashamedly rich it is, and even more so if served as a dessert with chocolate ice cream or lashings of whipped cream.

serves 12

you will need

400 g/14 oz good-quality plain chocolate, broken into pieces

400 g/14 oz butter, cut into cubes, plus extra for greasing

200 g/7 oz caster sugar

200 g/7 oz light soft brown sugar

200 g/7 oz plain white flour

6 large eggs

1 tsp vanilla extract

chocolate curls, to decorate

chocolate ice cream or whipped cream (optional), to serve

for the filling and topping

4 tbsp cocoa powder

4 tbsp boiling water

250 g/9 oz butter, softened

1 tsp vanilla extract

300 g/10½ oz icing sugar

1 Preheat the oven to 180°C/350°F/Gas Mark 4. Grease two 23 cm/9 in sandwich tins with butter and line with baking paper. Put the chocolate and butter in a large, heatproof bowl set over a saucepan of simmering water. Heat gently until smooth but not hot. Stir together and remove from the heat.

2 Using a wooden spoon, beat in the caster and brown sugar. Gradually stir in the flour. Beat the eggs and vanilla extract in a separate bowl, then beat well into the chocolate mixture. Turn the mixture into the prepared tins and spread out evenly.

3 Bake the cakes for about 40 minutes, or until a skewer inserted in the centre comes out clean. Leave to cool in the tin.

4 Meanwhile, make the filling and topping. Put the cocoa powder in a small bowl, add the boiling water and stir to form a smooth paste. Leave to cool. Put the butter and vanilla in a large bowl, sift in the icing sugar and beat with a wooden spoon until smooth. Beat in the cooled cocoa mixture.

5 When the cakes are cold, remove from the tins and sandwich together with half the filling. Swirl the remaining mixture over the top of the cake, then top with chocolate curls.

marble cake

It is fun to see the feathery swirls of this cake as you cut into it, and it is the attractive pattern, which looks similar in appearance to Italian marble, that gives this cake its name.

makes 9 squares

you will need

2 tbsp cocoa powder

2 tbsp water

175 g/6 oz butter or hard margarine, softened, plus extra for greasing

175 g/6 oz caster sugar

3 large eggs

200 g/7 oz white self-raising flour

2 tsp baking powder

1 tbsp milk

1 Preheat the oven to 180°C/350°F/Gas Mark 4. Grease a deep 20 cm/8 in cake tin with butter and line with baking paper. Put the cocoa powder and water in a large bowl and blend together until smooth.

2 Put the butter and sugar in a large bowl and, using an electric whisk, beat together until pale and fluffy. Beat the eggs in a bowl, then add to the mixture a little at a time, and beat together until incorporated.

3 Sift the flour and baking powder into the mixture and, using a large metal spoon, fold into the mixture, alternating with the milk, until combined.

4 Add half of the plain mixture into the cocoa mixture and stir together until well mixed.

5 Put large spoonfuls of the plain and chocolate mixture alternatively into the prepared tin. Draw a knife through the cake mixture in a spiral to create the marbled effect.

6 Bake the cake in the oven for 30–35 minutes, or until well risen and firm to the touch. Turn out of the tin and leave to cool on a wire rack.

devil's food cake

This dark, moist cake from America is filled and coated with a rich chocolate icing. It's probably because it's so wickedly sinful that it got its name. In America, it is often eaten as a dessert.

serves 8

you will need

115 g/4 oz butter or hard margarine, softened, plus extra for greasing

280 g/10 oz light soft brown sugar

2 large eggs

1 tsp vanilla extract

225 g/8 oz plain white flour

¼ tsp baking powder

1½ tsp bicarbonate of soda

40 g/1½ oz cocoa powder

225 ml/8 fl oz milk

for the icing

300 g/10½ oz granulated sugar

225 m/8 fl oz double cream

175 g/6 oz good-quality plain chocolate, grated

115 g/4 oz butter

1 Preheat the oven to 180°C/350°F/Gas Mark 4. Grease two 20 cm/8 in sandwich tins with butter and line with baking paper. Whisk the butter with half of the sugar in a large bowl.

2 Beat the eggs and vanilla extract together, and gradually beat into the mixture. Beat in the remaining sugar. Sift in the flour, baking powder, bicarbonate of soda and cocoa powder and fold in, alternating with the milk. Turn the mixture into the prepared tins and spread out evenly.

3 Bake the cakes in the oven for about 30 minutes, or until firm to the touch. Leave in the tins for 5 minutes to cool slightly, then turn out of the tins and leave to cool on a wire rack.

4 To make the icing, bring the sugar and cream to the boil in a heavy-based saucepan, stirring constantly. Reduce the heat and simmer for 10 minutes, without stirring. Remove from the heat, then stir in the chocolate and butter. Cool, then refrigerate, stirring occasionally, until spreadable.

5 Use a little icing to sandwich the cake halves together. Spread the remaining icing over the top and sides of the cake, pulling it into swirls to decorate. Leave to set before serving.

black forest gâteau

This traditional cake from Germany consists of a rich chocolate cake, moistened with kirsch syrup and filled and decorated with cherries and cream. It is a splendid cake to serve with coffee or as a dessert.

serves 8–10

you will need

175 g/6 oz butter, softened, plus extra for greasing

175 g/6 oz caster sugar

6 large eggs, separated

½ tsp vanilla extract

125 g/4½ oz white self-raising flour

75 g/2¾ oz cocoa powder

for the filling and topping

480 g/1 lb 1 oz frozen sweet, dark cherries

3 tbsp kirsch

425 ml/15 fl oz double cream

to decorate

50 g/1¾ oz plain chocolate curls

fresh cherries with their stalks, if in season

1 Preheat the oven to 180°C/350°F/Gas Mark 4. Grease a round, deep 23 cm/9 in cake tin with butter and line with baking paper. Put the butter and sugar in a large bowl and, using an electric whisk, beat together until pale and fluffy. Add the egg yolks and vanilla extract and beat together. Sift in the flour and cocoa powder and fold in. Whisk the egg whites until stiff, then fold in. Turn the mixture into the prepared tin.

2 Bake the cake for about 45 minutes, or until well risen and firm to the touch. Leave in the tin for 5 minutes to cool slightly, then turn out of the tin and leave to cool on a wire rack.

3 Meanwhile, allow the cherries to thaw, reserving 3 tablespoons of juice in a bowl. Add the kirsch to the reserved juices. Whisk the cream until it holds its shape. Cut the cake into three layers. Place one layer on a serving plate and spoon over 2 tablespoons of the kirsch syrup and spread with a little of the cream. Scatter over half the cherries. Repeat with the second and third layer but no cherries on the final layer.

4 Fill a piping bag, fitted with a large star nozzle, with the remaining cream and pipe around the edge of the cake. Decorate with chocolate curls, and fresh cherries if using.

chocolate brownies

You would be advised to find a good hiding place for these wonderful American chocolate cakes because they are guaranteed to disappear quickly. They are also good served with ice cream as a dessert.

makes 9 squares

you will need

115 g/4 oz walnuts

175 g/6 oz good-quality plain chocolate

175 g/6 oz butter, cut into cubes, plus extra for greasing

3 large eggs

1 tsp vanilla extract

250 g/9 oz caster sugar

115 g/4 oz plain white flour

icing sugar, to decorate

1 Preheat the oven to 180°C/350°F/Gas Mark 4. Grease a square 20 cm/8 in cake tin with butter and line with baking paper. Roughly chop the walnuts.

2 Break the chocolate into a large, heavy-based saucepan. Add the butter and heat gently until the butter has melted and the ingredients are runny but not hot. Stir together until combined. Remove from the heat.

3 Beat the eggs, vanilla extract and sugar together in a large bowl. When the chocolate mixture has cooled slightly, add to the egg mixture and beat together.

4 Add the flour and, using a large metal spoon, fold into the mixture. Add the chopped walnuts and stir together until combined. Turn the mixture into the prepared tin.

5 Bake the cake in the oven for about 45 minutes, or until the top is firm but the centre just set. The mixture should still wobble slightly in the centre. Do not overcook because it will continue to cook slightly as it cools. Leave to cool in the tin before cutting into squares. Dust with sifted icing sugar to decorate before serving.

chocolate crispy cakes

These little uncooked cakes are associated with children, but adults love them too. If making them for a birthday, add candles or, at Easter time, add a few chocolate speckled eggs to decorate before they set.

you will need

200 g/7 oz good-quality plain chocolate

100 g/3½ oz butter

175 g/6 oz golden syrup

150 g/5½ oz cornflakes

1 Place 12 fluted paper or foil baking cases on a baking tray. Break the chocolate into a large, heavy-based saucepan.

2 Add the butter and golden syrup to the saucepan. Heat gently until the butter has melted and the ingredients are runny but not hot. Stir together until combined.

3 Add the cornflakes to the saucepan and stir together until well mixed.

4 Spoon the mixture evenly into the paper cases and leave to set before serving.

lemon polenta cake

Italy is the home of the stylish polenta cake. It is delicious served with coffee or as a dessert with fresh fruit and cream and, should you wish to add a little luxury, this recipe has the addition of Limoncello liqueur.

serves 8–10

you will need

4 large lemons

225 g/8 oz butter or hard margarine, softened, plus extra for greasing

225 g/8 oz caster sugar

6 large eggs, separated

175 g/6 oz ground almonds

100 g/3½ oz polenta

2 tbsp Limoncello liqueur (optional)

icing sugar, to decorate

1 Preheat the oven to 180°C/350°F/Gas Mark 4. Grease a 23 cm/9 in spring-release cake tin with butter and line with baking paper. Finely grate the rind and squeeze the juice of the lemons.

2 Put the butter and sugar in a large bowl and, using an electric whisk, beat together until pale and fluffy. Add the egg yolks and beat together.

3 Add the ground almonds, polenta, lemon rind and juice to the mixture and beat together until well mixed.

4 Whisk the egg whites until stiff and then, using a large metal spoon, fold into the mixture until combined. Turn the mixture into the prepared tin and spread out evenly.

5 Bake the cake in the oven for 50–60 minutes, or until golden brown and firm to the touch. If wished, when the cake is cooked, spoon the Limoncello evenly over the hot cake and leave to cool in the tin before removing. When cold, dust the cake with sifted icing sugar, to decorate.

almond apple cake

This moist cake is so delicious that you will find yourself making it time and time again. It is also inexpensive because it doesn't contain ground almonds – it gets its flavour from the addition of almond extract.

serves 8–10

you will need

150 g/5½ oz butter or hard margarine, softened, plus extra for greasing

225 g/8 oz caster sugar

2 large eggs

1 tsp almond extract

225 g/8 oz self-raising white flour

1½ tsp baking powder

1 large or 2 small cooking apples

50 g/1¾ oz flaked almonds

1 Preheat the oven to 150°C/300°F/Gas Mark 2. Grease a 23 cm/ 9 in round, loose-bottomed cake tin with butter and line with baking paper. Put the butter and sugar in a large bowl and, using an electric whisk, beat together until pale and fluffy.

2 Beat the eggs in a small bowl, then add to the mixture with the almond extract and beat together until incorporated.

3 Sift the flour and baking powder into the bowl, then mix together. Spread half the mixture into the prepared tin.

4 Peel and thinly slice the apples and place the slices in a layer on top of the cake mixture in the tin.

5 Spoon the remaining cake mixture over the apple slices and spread out evenly. Sprinkle the almonds on top to decorate.

6 Bake the cake in the oven for 1–1¼ hours, or until golden brown and a skewer inserted in the centre comes out clean. Leave to cool in the tin before removing.

banana teabread

Instead of the more usual addition of walnuts, sweet buttery Brazil nuts combine beautifully with the bananas to produce this moist teabread. Serve spread with butter to give it an added sumptuousness.

serves 10–12

you will need

115 g/4 oz Brazil nuts

450 g/1 lb bananas

2 large eggs

200 g/7 oz white self-raising flour

¼ tsp bicarbonate of soda

85 g/3 oz butter or hard margarine, softened, plus extra for greasing

175 g/6 oz caster sugar

butter, to serve

1 Preheat the oven to 180°C/350°F/Gas Mark 4. Grease a 900 g/ 2 lb loaf tin with butter and line with baking paper. Roughly chop the Brazil nuts. Put the bananas in a large bowl and mash with a fork. Add the eggs and beat together until smooth.

2 Sift the flour and bicarbonate of soda together into a large bowl. Add the butter and rub in with your fingers until the mixture resembles fine breadcrumbs. Alternatively, put the flour, bicarbonate of soda and the butter in a food processor and blend together, using a pulsating action, to form fine breadcrumbs.

3 Stir the chopped nuts and sugar into the mixture. Add the banana mixture and stir together until well mixed. Turn the mixture into the prepared tin and spread out evenly.

4 Bake the cake for about 1¼ hours, or until golden brown and firm to the touch. Leave in the tin for 5 minutes to cool slightly, then turn out of the tin and leave to cool on a wire rack.

5 Ideally, wrap in baking paper and then in foil and store in an airtight container for 1 day to mature. Slice and spread with butter, to serve.

fresh orange cake

Bursting with the flavour of fresh oranges, this delicious cake is rather sophisticated but surprisingly easy to make. It is therefore ideal to make when you want to impress your guests.

you will need

2 large oranges

250 g/9 oz butter or hard margarine, softened, plus extra for greasing

250 g/9 oz caster sugar

4 large eggs

250 g/9 oz self-raising white flour

1 tsp baking powder

1 Preheat the oven to 160°C/325°F/Gas Mark 3. Grease a 23 cm/ 9 in loose-bottomed cake tin with butter and line with baking paper. Peel one orange and cut into quarters, then blend in a food processor until finely chopped. Turn into a bowl. Squeeze the juice from the remaining orange into the bowl and set aside.

2 Put the butter and 200 g/7 oz of the sugar in a large bowl and, using an electric whisk, beat together until pale and fluffy. Beat the eggs in a small bowl, then add to the mixture a little at a time, and beat together until incorporated.

3 Sift the flour and baking powder into the bowl. Add the reserved chopped orange and 2 tablespoons of the orange juice, then beat together until well mixed. Turn the mixture into the prepared tin and spread out evenly.

4 Bake the cake in the oven for 1¼–1½ hours, or until golden brown and firm to the touch.

5 Meanwhile, make the syrup. Add the remaining 50 g/1¾ oz sugar to the remaining orange juice. Stir until the sugar has dissolved. When the cake is cooked, spoon the syrup evenly over the hot cake. Leave to cool in the tin before removing.

lemon drizzle cake

Clean-tasting lemon drizzle cake is the classic cake made for fêtes, school fundraising events, coffee mornings across the country, and any other occasion when a nice home-made cake is required.

serves 8–10

you will need

115 g/4 oz butter or hard margarine, softened, plus extra for greasing

175 g/6 oz caster sugar

2 large eggs

1 large lemon

175 g/6 oz self-raising white flour

4 tbsp milk

60 g/2¼ oz icing sugar

1 Preheat the oven to 180°C/350°F/Gas Mark 4. Grease a 900 g/2 lb loaf tin with butter and line with baking paper. Put the butter and caster sugar in a large bowl and, using an electric whisk, beat together until pale and fluffy.

2 Beat the eggs in a small bowl, then add to the mixture a little at a time, and beat together until incorporated.

3 Finely grate the lemon rind into the mixture. Add the flour and milk and beat together until well mixed. Turn the mixture into the prepared tin and spread out evenly.

4 Bake the cake in the oven for 35–40 minutes, or until a skewer inserted in the centre comes out clean.

5 Meanwhile, squeeze the juice from the lemon and pour into a bowl. Add the icing sugar and stir together until the sugar has dissolved. When the cake is cooked, spoon the syrup evenly over the hot cake and leave to cool in the tin before turning out.

raspberry streusel cake

It is the buttery, crumbly streusel topping that gives this subtly spiced fruit cake its lovely texture. This mouthwatering cake will give your household an added treat to spice up the weekend.

serves 8–10

you will need

150 g/5 oz butter, softened, plus extra for greasing

150 g/5 oz caster sugar

1 large egg

100 g/3½ oz ground almonds

150 g/5½ oz self-raising white flour

1 tsp ground cinnamon

225 g/8 oz fresh raspberries, plus extra to serve

whipped double cream, to serve

for the topping

75 g/2¾ oz plain white flour

½ tsp ground cinnamon

40 g/1½ oz butter, cut into cubes

75 g/2¾ oz Demerara sugar

25 g/1 oz flaked almonds

1   Preheat the oven to 180°C/350°F/Gas Mark 4. Grease and line a 23 cm/9 in round, loose-bottomed cake tin. For the topping, sift the flour and cinnamon together into a large bowl. Rub in the butter with your fingers until the mixture resembles fine breadcrumbs. Alternatively, put the flour, cinnamon and butter in a food processor and blend, using a pulsating action, to form fine breadcrumbs. Stir in the sugar and flaked almonds.

2   To make the cake, put the butter and sugar in a large bowl and, using an electric whisk, beat until pale and fluffy. Beat the egg in a small bowl, then add to the mixture with the ground almonds, and beat together until incorporated. Sift the flour and cinnamon together into the mixture and, using a large metal spoon, fold in until incorporated. Turn half the cake mixture into the prepared tin and level the surface. Scatter over the raspberries, then spoon over the remaining cake mixture to cover the raspberries and spread out evenly. Sprinkle over the topping mixture.

3   Bake the cake for 1–1¼ hours, or until golden brown and firm to the touch. Leave to cool in the tin before removing. Serve with raspberries and cream.

vanilla sponge cake

Layers of moist vanilla cake filled with strawberries and cream look stunning, so this is a cake to make for a special occasion and when fresh strawberries are in season.

serves 10

you will need

225 g/8 oz butter, plus extra for greasing

350 g/12 oz caster sugar

5 large eggs

2 tsp vanilla extract

350 g/12 oz plain white flour

2 tsp baking powder

100 ml/3½ fl oz milk

400 g/14 oz fresh strawberries

425 ml/15 fl oz double cream

Icing sugar, to decorate

1 Preheat the oven to 180°C/350°F/Gas Mark 4. Grease two 23 cm/9 in sandwich tins with butter and line with baking paper. Put the butter and sugar in a large bowl and, using an electric whisk, beat together until pale and fluffy. Beat the eggs and vanilla together, and gradually beat into the mixture. Sift in the flour and baking powder and fold in, alternating with the milk until combined. Turn the mixture into the prepared tins and spread out evenly.

2 Bake the cakes for 35–40 minutes, or until golden brown and firm to the touch. Leave in the tins for 5 minutes to cool, then turn out of the tins and leave to cool on a wire rack. When the cakes are cold, cut each into two layers. Put one layer on a serving plate. Thinly slice the strawberries, reserving 10 to decorate.

3 Whisk the cream until stiff. Spread a third of the cream over the bottom layer of cake and top with the second layer. Add the sliced strawberries. Top with the third sponge layer, then spread over a third of the cream and top with the fourth layer. Fill a piping bag, fitted with a large star nozzle, with the remaining cream and pipe around the top edge of the cake. Decorate with the reserved strawberries and dust with sifted icing sugar.

cherry cake

Often the problem with cherry cakes is that the cherries sink to the bottom of the cake. The problem is avoided in this cake recipe because they are arranged in the bottom of the tin before it is baked!

serves 10

you will need

70 g/2½ oz self-raising white flour

350 g/12 oz glacé cherries

225 g/8 oz butter or hard margarine, softened, plus extra for greasing

225 g/8 oz caster sugar

6 large eggs

½ tsp almond extract

175 g/6 oz ground almonds

icing sugar, to decorate

1 Preheat the oven to 180°C/350°F/Gas Mark 4. Grease a 23 cm/ 9 in deep, round, loose-bottomed cake tin with butter and line with baking paper. Spread the flour on a large plate. Toss the cherries in it to dust lightly, then arrange the cherries in a single layer in the bottom of the prepared tin. Set aside the remaining flour.

2 Put the butter and sugar in a large bowl and, using an electric whisk, beat together until pale and fluffy.

3 Beat the eggs in a bowl, then add to the mixture a little at a time with the almond extract, and beat together until incorporated.

4 Add the remaining flour and the ground almonds to the mixture and fold in until well combined. Turn the mixture on top of the cherries in the tin.

5 Bake the cake in the preheated oven for 1 hour, or until golden brown and a skewer inserted in the centre comes out clean. Leave to cool in the tin before removing.

6 When the cake is cold, remove from the tin and dust with sifted icing sugar to decorate.

decorating ideas

The decoration really is 'the icing on the cake'. Sometimes a simple dusting of sifted icing sugar is all that is necessary. On other occasions a whirl of butter cream or smooth coating of glacé icing adds a finishing touch.

A basic butter cream icing consists of 85 g/3 oz butter, 175 g/ 6 oz icing sugar, 1–2 tablespoons milk and a few drops of vanilla extract. For chocolate butter cream, dissolve 2 tablespoons cocoa powder in a little hot water and cool before adding to the mixture. This is sufficient to cover and fill an 18 cm/7 in diameter cake. Simply spread and swirl or pipe the icing on top of the cake to decorate.

A glacé icing consists of 115 g/4 oz icing sugar, and 1 tablespoon warm water or strained fresh fruit juice. Add the liquid gradually so that it is thick enough to coat the back of the spoon. If necessary, add more water or sugar to adjust the consistency. For chocolate glacé icing, dissolve 2 teaspoons cocoa powder in a little hot water and use instead of the same amount of water. This is sufficient to cover a 20 cm/8 in diameter cake. If icing both the top and sides of a cake, stand it on a wire rack, over a tray to catch any drips, before transferring it to a serving plate. Use the icing as soon as it has been made and add any decoration before the icing sets.

Keep a supply of ready-made decorations in the store cupboard so that a cake can be made at a moment's notice. These include silver and gold dragées (balls), chocolate-coated coffee beans and, for children, chocolate-coated sweets, hundreds

and thousands, and sugar decorations. Ingredients include nuts, particularly flaked almonds, blanched almonds and walnuts, glacé cherries, plain chocolate for making chocolate curls, chocolate flake and, of course, icing sugar for giving the cake a liberal dusting.

Finally, don't forget to keep a supply of cake candles and, for a change from the usual birthday cake, add candles to a collection of individual small cakes to serve on that special occasion. Then all you need to do is stand back and enjoy the fruits of your labours as the candles are blown out.

index

acknowledgements

Baltic Trader,
The Old Needlemakers,
West Street,
Lewes,
East Sussex
BN7 2NZ
(www.baltictrader.co.uk)

Monsieur Canelle
et Compagnon,
The Old Needlemakers,
West Street,
Lewes,
East Sussex
BN7 2NZ

Steamer Trading,
20/21 High Street,
Lewes,
East Sussex
BN7 2BY